*Greater Than a Tourist I
Ebook and Audiobook form

Greater Than a Tourist Book Series
Reviews from Readers

I think the series is wonderful and beneficial for tourists to get information before visiting the city.

-Seckin Zumbul, Izmir Turkey

I am a world traveler who has read many trip guides but this one really made a difference for me. I would call it a heartfelt creation of a local guide expert instead of just a guide.

-Susy, Isla Holbox, Mexico

New to the area like me, this is a must have!

 -Joe, Bloomington, USA

This is a good series that gets down to it when looking for things to do at your destination without having to read a novel for just a few ideas.

-Rachel, Monterey, USA

Good information to have to plan my trip to this destination.

-Pennie Farrell, Mexico

Great ideas for a port day.

-Mary Martin USA

Aptly titled, you won't just be a tourist after reading this book. You'll be greater than a tourist!

-Alan Warner, Grand Rapids, USA

Even though I only have three days to spend in San Miguel in an upcoming visit, I will use the author's suggestions to guide some of my time there. An easy read - with chapters named to guide me in directions I want to go.

-Robert Catapano, USA

Great insights from a local perspective! Useful information and a very good value!

-Sarah, USA

This series provides an in-depth experience through the eyes of a local. Reading these series will help you to travel the city in with confidence and it'll make your journey a unique one.

-Andrew Teoh, Ipoh, Malaysia

\>TOURIST

GREATER THAN A TOURIST-OHRID MACEDONIA

50 Travel Tips from a Local

Marina Ivanovska

Greater Than a Tourist-Ohrid Macedonia Copyright © 2020 by CZYK Publishing LLC. All Rights Reserved.

All rights reserved. No part of this book may be reproduced in any form or by any electronic or mechanical means including information storage and retrieval systems, without permission in writing from the author. The only exception is by a reviewer, who may quote short excerpts in a review.

The statements in this book are of the authors and may not be the views of CZYK Publishing or Greater Than a Tourist.

First Edition

Cover designed by: Ivana Stamenkovic

Cover Image: https://pixabay.com/photos/ohrid-town-city-harbor-lake-water-3299816/

Image 1: https://en.wikipedia.org/wiki/File8F.jpg Михал Орела / CC BY (https://creativecommons.org/licenses/by/2.0)

Image 2: https://en.wikipedia.org/wiki/File:Ohrid_by_night.jpg Shermozle / CC BY-SA (http://creativecommons.org/licenses/by-sa/3.0/)

Image 3: https://en.wikipedia.org/wiki/File:Sv.Bogorodica_Perivlepta-1.jpg Slavica Panova / CC BY-SA (https://creativecommons.org/licenses/by-sa/3.0)

Image 4: https://en.wikipedia.org/wiki/File:%D0%9F%D0%BB%D0%B0%D0%BE%D1%88%D0%BD%D0%B8%D0%BA_-_%D0%9E%D1%85%D1%80%D0%B8%D0%B4_1.jpg MadMona / CC BY-SA (https://creativecommons.org/licenses/by-sa/4.0)

CZYK Publishing Since 2011.
Greater Than a Tourist

Lock Haven, PA
All rights reserved.

ISBN: 9798632554626

>TOURIST

>TOURIST
50 TRAVEL TIPS FROM A LOCAL

BOOK DESCRIPTION

With travel tips and culture in our guidebooks written by a local author, it is never too late to visit Ohrid. Greater Than a Tourist - Ohrid, Macedonia by Marina Ivanovska offers the inside scoop on Ohrid, the city of pearls. Most travel books tell you how to travel like a tourist. Although there is nothing wrong with that, as part of the 'Greater Than a Tourist' series, this book will give you candid travel tips from someone who has lived at your next travel destination. This guide book will not tell you exact addresses or store hours but instead gives you knowledge that you may not find in other smaller print travel books. Experience cultural, culinary delights, and attractions with the guidance of a Local. Slow down and get to know the people with this invaluable guide. By the time you finish this book, you will be eager and prepared to discover new activities at your next travel destination.

Inside this travel guide book you will find:

Visitor information from a Local
Tour ideas and inspiration
Save time with valuable guidebook information

Greater Than a Tourist- A Travel Guidebook with 50 Travel Tips from a Local. Slow down, stay in one place, and get to know the people and culture. By the time you finish this book, you will be eager and prepared to travel to your next destination.

OUR STORY

Traveling is a passion of the Greater than a Tourist book series creator. Lisa studied abroad in college, and for their honeymoon Lisa and her husband toured Europe. During her travels to Malta, an older man tried to give her some advice based on his own experience living on the island since he was a young boy. She was not sure if she should talk to the stranger but was interested in his advice. When traveling to some places she was wary to talk to locals because she was afraid that they weren't being genuine. Through her travels, Lisa learned how much locals had to share with tourists. Lisa created the Greater Than a Tourist book series to help connect people with locals. A topic that locals are very passionate about sharing.

>TOURIST

TABLE OF CONTENTS

BOOK DESCRIPTION
OUR STORY
TABLE OF CONTENTS
DEDICATION
ABOUT THE AUTHOR
HOW TO USE THIS BOOK
FROM THE PUBLISHER
WELCOME TO > TOURIST
1. History Of Ohrid
2. Common Courtesies
3. Best Times To Visit
4. Currency To Carry
5. If You Don't Find Accommodation, The Accommodation Will Find You
6. How To Get Around
7. Where To Walk
8. Where To Bicycle
9. Where To Bike
10. Where To Drive
11. Where To Boat
12. Where To Coffee
13. Have A Snack On The Way
14. Sweeten your tooth
15. Street Food

16. Buy Some Groceries
17. The Burek Chronicles
18. What To Have For Breakfast
19. I Bet You'll Bet
20. As Safe As Houses
21. Still Not Safe For The LGBTQ
22. Wear Whatever You Like
23. Internet And Network
24. Social Websites To Follow For Local News
25. Radio Culture
26. Music – What's Popular?
27. Art – What's Popular?
28. Jewelry – What's Popular?
29. The Almighty Pearl
30. Shopping Culture
31. Take A Swim
32. Taxi And Other Transport
33. Public Holidays
34. Parties
35. Experience The Lake – Rent a Kayak
36. What To Take With You - Clothes
37. What To Take With You - Items
38. What To Photograph
39. Festivals
40. Sports
41. Experience The Mountains - Hike

>TOURIST

42. If You Get Up Early
43. An Idea If You Want To Take A Swim
44. Where Is The Most Breathtaking View
45. Vodici – the most important day for locals
46. Explore The Neighbourhood
47. The Village With Its Own Passport
48. Museums
49. Visit The Fishermen
50. Never Get Sick Again – The Happy Meal For Grown-ups

TOP REASONS TO BOOK THIS TRIP

Other Resources:

Packing and Planning Tips

Travel Questions

Travel Bucket List

NOTES

>TOURIST

DEDICATION

This book is dedicated to my future nephew, who is 7 months into making. May you find joy in these places when you grow up, just like I have.

ABOUT THE AUTHOR

Marina is a copywriter and hotel owner who lives in Ohrid, Macedonia and loves to eat her boyfriends' cooked dinners.

She loves to travel and visit her second home in Sydney, and she memorizes the places she visited by smell.

Marina has lived in Ohrid for 29 years – since she was born. She lived in Skopje, the main city in Macedonia when she was at university, and she remembers those 5 years as great, but missing the smell of pine trees and water – the smell of Ohrid.

>TOURIST

HOW TO USE THIS BOOK

The *Greater Than a Tourist* book series was written by someone who has lived in an area for over three months. The goal of this book is to help travelers either dream or experience different locations by providing opinions from a local. The author has made suggestions based on their own experiences. Please check before traveling to the area in case the suggested places are unavailable.

Travel Advisories: As a first step in planning any trip abroad, check the Travel Advisories for your intended destination.
https://travel.state.gov/content/travel/en/traveladvisories/traveladvisories.html

\>TOURIST

FROM THE PUBLISHER

Traveling can be one of the most important parts of a person's life. The anticipation and memories that you have are some of the best. As a publisher of the Greater Than a Tourist, as well as the popular *50 Things to Know* book series, we strive to help you learn about new places, spark your imagination, and inspire you. Wherever you are and whatever you do I wish you safe, fun, and inspiring travel.

Lisa Rusczyk Ed. D.
CZYK Publishing

>TOURIST

WELCOME TO
> TOURIST

>TOURIST

Ohrid and Lake Ohrid

Ohrid by night. The ancient name of the city was Lychnidos, which probably means "city of light"

Mother of God Perybleptos church, located across the icon gallery

Archeological site of Plaosnik

>TOURIST

What possessed force to attract me, it did, it beat me, and for hours for days and nights, I could not leave the coast of the Ohrid Lake.

- Branislav Nushic (Serbian writer 1894)

Ohrid is a beautiful city in the heart of the Balkan peninsula, in a small and sunny country called Macedonia. Ohrid is the main tourist city in Macedonia, and rightfully so.

Sea-like lake and beautiful old-timey architecture are surrounded by the most statuesque mountains.

Those mountains hold a lot of tiny gems hidden in this small pearl of a city.

As a local, I will share my secrets with you, so you can experience my city as if you were born here.

Ohrid
North Macedonia

Ohrid Climate

	High	Low
January	43	29
February	46	30
March	53	35
April	60	41
May	71	48
June	79	54
July	83	57
August	83	57
September	74	52
October	64	45
November	53	37
December	45	32

GreaterThanaTourist.com

Temperatures are in Fahrenheit degrees.
Source: NOAA

1. History Of Ohrid

Ohrid, with its natural, cultural, spiritual and historical features, is the most developed tourist and cultural center, not only in the Republic of Macedonia but in the Balkans and beyond in Europe and the World. These values have been recognized by the world as well, so Ohrid and Lake Ohrid, as a rare cultural and natural heritage, are on the UNESCO list. One powerful information is the claim of the world scientific community that Ohrid has a continuous life of 7000 years, and the remains of civilizations are visible in over 250 archeological sites discovered so far.

Ohrid is also the center of Christianity of all Slavs, the seat of the Archbishopric, the first schools and universities in this area and beyond. Today Ohrid is the center of world archeological discoveries and sites. Ohrid is the city of 365 churches. One church for each day of the year.

2. Common Courtesies

Ohrid is a multicultural city where the natives are from different backgrounds. The main two religions are Christian Orthodox and Muslim.

We live in a peaceful community and extreme religious groups are not a part of our everyday lives, but educating on the common courtesies when entering a religious building is very welcomed.

Don't be loud, don't bring in snacks, and always ask the people who work there if you are allowed to take photos inside.

3. Best Times To Visit

Ohrid is a wonderful and scenic city all year round, but you should know that you will have a very different experience depending on the season you're visiting.

If you ask any native person, including me, we will tell you that the best time to visit is in Spring or Fall. We are a sunny country and because of the amazing nature, you will have time and privacy to enjoy all the hidden gems that Ohrid has to offer.

In the summer, on the other hand – that is when all the tourists come and Ohrid looks like Ibiza's little brother. The summer months are hot, but not steaming – the temperatures go up to 87-88 Fahrenheit and sunbathing and swimming is very pleasant. All the parties and festivities take place in July and August, so if you like to party – come then!

Winters are typically calm and they don't offer almost any events. Young people migrate to Skopje as it is the main center for education and work, so we would recommend Ohrid in winter for the elderly.

4. Currency To Carry

A very nice tip to have in mind when it comes to currency is that every exchange office has the same rate. You don't have to worry about finding an exchange office that will steal 20 percent more than the next one.

Our local currency is the Macedonian Denar – and don't mistake it with the Serbian Dinar – as they are quite different. In 2020, the Denar-Dinar ratio is 1:2.

You can bring your local currency but have in mind that if you live in a more exotic country, there is a possibility that your currency won't be accepted.

The Euro, American Dollar, Australian Dollar, Canadian Dollar, The Pound Sterling, Swiss franc, Turkish Lira, Hungarian forint, and the currencies from the neighborhood countries – Albanian Lek, Serbian Dinar, Croatian Kuna – are surely going to be accepted in any exchange office in Ohrid.

The best way to pay is by Denars, or with a credit card.

Some places will not accept credit cards, as they are registered as craftsmen, to avoid unnecessary taxes that will leave the owners of small businesses without any earnings.

5. IF YOU DON'T FIND ACCOMMODATION, THE ACCOMMODATION WILL FIND YOU

As the main tourist city, Ohrid can give you a plethora of accommodation options. It all depends on your liking.

5-star hotels, private accommodations, villas in the center, hostels and motels are all part of the great organism that is Ohrid tourism.

Don't be alarmed if people offering an accommodation approach you on the street when you park your car or look at the map. It is a part of the system, the people who usually work on the parking lots or some paid "agents" on bikes offer you a nice hotel to stay in or a private room, as they are paid some percent of the earnings if they convince you to stay at the said hotel. This is NOT a scam. They are simply a

>TOURIST

walking commercial for the crazy amount of accommodation there is available in Ohrid.

However, we DO NOT advise you to come to Ohrid without a pre-booked place. The possibility to find somewhere to sleep is big, but if you hit a good-weather weekend or public holiday, then there is a great chance that you'll sleep in the park.

6. How To Get Around

Ohrid with its 383.9 km^2 (148.2 sq miles) is one of those cities that is just a sin if you try to see it inside a car or a bus. Although there are taxis everywhere, and there are places that you will need a vehicle to go to and see, the majority of Ohrid is completely walkable.

Another great idea if you don't want to walk everywhere is to rent a Bike or nowadays commonly popular – the electric scooter.

A popular way of experiencing the city is by little boats that are everywhere on the coast. Experienced sailors will tell you all about the history of Ohrid, and are filled with city trivia that will keep you amused. If that doesn't work, they will often offer you a national alcoholic drink called – Rakia, and everything will become more interesting.

7. Where To Walk

Let's say you get to the main square, and you want to know which way to head next. There are three paths that you can take – right, left, and back if you are facing the lake.

If you go to the right, it means you chose the road that will take you to the old part of the town filled with little museums such as The House of Robevci, The Papirus museum and a lot of little workshops whose owners specialize in handmade filigree and wood carving. The most popular church Saint John of Kaneo is that way, the Samoil Fortress from the 4th Century B.C., the Ancient Theater from the 200 BC, and the amazing Church of Saint Sophia, and they are all pretty close to each other. Among these amazing buildings, you will find a few very nice restaurants, lounge bars, and a few clubs where you can stop, take a rest, fill your batteries and enjoy the lake view.

If you take the left side, then you've decided to take a stroll by the lakeside. You'll likely encounter beautiful swans and other lake birds that will come to greet you and maybe have a bite from your snacks. You can continue to walk by the lake for a few minutes and on your way, you'll see a few nice restaurants, and two if the most famous pubs – Irish pub and Tino's.

Let's say you decided to turn your back on the lake and head down the old shopping street, also called Carsija (pronounced char-shee-yah). A lot of high-quality jewelry, perfume and clothing shops will come your way. If you want to buy your groceries on the local farmers market, famously called Pazar (bazaar), and visit the 1000-year-old tree called Chinar, then head this way, too.

8. Where To Bicycle

You can rent a bike in almost every hotel in the city, also in the car rentals and tourist agencies. The bike rentals are weirdly expensive, for about 10-15 euros a day, but they will make the investment worth it.

If you lack stamina, you can bike down the lake and visit the Cuba Libre beach club, have a coffee or a cold beer there and have the whole city in your eyesight.

If you want to break a sweat you can continue biking on the trail until you meet the Ohrid coast again. This end of the road is also the beginning point of a group of famous beaches called Goritsa Three. They are considered to be the most famous for family swim days as the coast is shallow and the rocks are not sharp.

9. Where To Bike

If you are not a part of a cool biker gang and you don't own a Harley Davidson and a great leather jacket with fringe, then you can take your 10-year-old windbreaker and rent a motorbike from the same places you would rent a car. There is a lot of information online for car and bike rentals, so I don't need to endorse any particular one.

Take your bike and have a drive that is 30 km (18.6 miles) long, heading to the Albanian border called Tushemisht. May your first stop be the nearest village called Peshtani. It is a great coastal village and offers great pizzerias and fish. The local fish is a trout, called Pastrmka, and Peshtani is one of the villages that has the best fish. The villagers are considered to be feisty, fast-talking and weirdly taller than the Ohridians. After that, visit the Bay of the Bones, an archeological complex located at the excavation site and it is an authentic reconstruction of the pile dwelling settlement. After this 16km (9.9 miles) mark, continue to Gradishte beach if it's swim season, if not, bike away to the

>TOURIST

village of Trpejca, another beautiful coastal village that looks like a multi-million dollar escape destination in Northern Italy, but with cows and fishermen.

After Trpejca, one famous beach/village for the Ohrid natives is Ljubanishta, but they don't want you to know this as they get away here from the crowded city in July, August, and September.

Finish your 30 km (18.6 miles) journey as you arrive in the Saint Naum village. Beautiful monasteries, beaches, restaurants, and peacocks will make your eyes water. You must park your motorbike here and take a little boat ride with a local guide around the springs, who will tell you everything there's to know.

10. Where To Drive

If you have a car you can take a day trip to the top of the most famous mountain called Galicica (gah-lee-tschee-tsuh), and park at the famous 2250 meter peak Magaro from where you can see the two most famous lakes in Macedonia – the Ohrid Lake and the Prespa Lake.

If you want to head to the opposite way of the lake, you can head to the nearest city called Struga or see the amazing village called Vevchani, which has a lot of amazing little homely restaurants and it's the home of the popular Vevcani carnival on every 13th of January, also known as the old orthodox calendar's New year. The carnival is satirical, and it lasts two days, oftentimes filled with parties, alcohol and traditional and modern live music performances.

11. Where To Boat

The most famous boat in Ohrid is called Alexandria. It's a company that owns two boats who sail every day from 10 pm and can take you around the lake, or 'give you a lift' to St. Naum and take you back in three hours.

On the Ohrid Lake coast in the center, you will see a lot of small flat white boats called Catamarans, which cost around 250 euros and can sit up to 15 people. They are a little bit more expensive than the regular little boats or the biggest ones like the Alexandria, that will have you pay 10 euros for a round trip to Saint Naum and back.

12. Where To Coffee

Ohrid is a place where you can get a coffee every 20 meters. The most popular coffee in every household is

>TOURIST

the Turkish, black coffee, drunk by every woman and man in the early morning to boost the energy. It is considered to be the healthiest and most effective.

People usually drink macchiatos and espressos, and nowadays you can get a cold brew and drip coffee in the center, in healthy food takeaway places like Shilla and Fruit box, located on the main street Carsija. Besides the biggest supermarkets, there is only one specialized private shop for freshly ground coffee, located next to the old tree Cinar in the little Turkish Carsija.

13. Have A Snack On The Way

Don't walk empty-bellied. Ohrid is a small and beautiful city that you have an impression you can fit in your pocket, but you can easily wander around the old hills or the coast, and next thing you know, the sun has set and you are tired and hungry. A very common thing the natives do is they take pumpkin or sunflower seeds and just snack away while having a friendly walk with their close ones. You can visit the health store called Bako, located at the start of the Carsija, and choose a healthy (or not so healthy) snack, from peanuts to chocolate, Kombucha or Coca-Cola.

14. Sweeten your tooth

Macedonian cuisine is tightly influenced by Turkish food, as we were under the rule of the Ottoman Empire for 5 centuries. The tastiest example of this influence is arguably the presence of a lot of amazing patisseries and dessert shops, where you can order baklava, tulumba, kadaif, and other sherbet desserts, along with popular cakes as black forest, cheesecake, fruit, and chocolate cake.

Take a walk on the short Turkish street left of the Cinar tree and have baklava and Turkish tea there, have a delicious Ohrid cake (with walnuts and caramel) in Palma, eat ice-cream at Korzo or Letnica, or have a high quality, luxurious and little bit pricey-but-never-forgettable cake in cake shop Ljushe.

15. Street Food

The culture of street food has changed in recent years as people have started to look for higher quality food that will give you a more unique and unforgettable experience.

>TOURIST

The most popular burger place in the center is called Burger Station, located in the center of Carsija. They serve high-quality beef meat in their burgers, give you baked potatoes instead of fries and make their mayonnaise-like sauce in their home.

Without a doubt, the most popular place for locals and tourists to go to when they want to eat high-quality food for a low price is down the Turkish Carsija. It is located left of the Old Cinar tree and it is very short but packed with culture and flavor. Rotisserie chicken, baked beans and kebabs are all part of the menu, and they offer you an unforgettable flavor. Don't miss going to Vkusno (Tasty), a Turkish restaurant specializing in small kebabs.

There is a Greek influence in the summer street food vendors as you can often find giro places, and also the occasional pizza slice for one euro is quite welcomed, as it is quite tasty and easy on the stomach.

16. Buy Some Groceries

For quite a small town Ohrid is very rich with supermarkets and local grocery shops who offer great products for reasonable prices. In the main square, there are two biggest supermarkets called Tinex and Ramstore – the latter works until later and it is a little bit pricier.

The cheapest supermarket is called Kam, it is located near the Bazaar and it famously never plays music inside. Although it is the cheapest one, it oftentimes has the most interesting products that you cannot find in any other commercial market.

17. The Burek Chronicles

It is 3 am. You just called it a night and you are leaving from the most popular Jazz and Blues Cabaret, tipsy and quite hungry. Your stomach is growling and you are standing in the main square, seeing that the supermarkets are closed. But you can smell something divine. What is it? It's the pastry street. Down the main street with the shops (Carsija), there is a parallel road for the cars. Down that road, there are a few 24-hour pastry shops. Even if you are not hungry. Just go inside. Smell. And BUY BUREK. With meat or cheese. Get yogurt. Taste paradise.

18. What To Have For Breakfast

>TOURIST

If you want to have breakfast as a regular Ohridian, then hit the pastry shops. The most popular light breakfast is just having a savory round pastry called Gevrek resembling the German pretzel. Often the burek and little cup of local yogurt is a hearty and tasty breakfast choice.

If you want something healthier and don't want to eat sitting in a restaurant, then take a muesli cup in Steve's coffee shop by the Ohrid coast or pick an amazing tasting smoothie at Fruitbox.

Ohrid people usually eat beef, chicken or fish stew in the mornings at the weekends, and elderly people love to eat garlic EVERY MORNING, so don't be surprised if you often smell the unmistakable smell of garlic around you.

19. I Bet You'll Bet

Where there is a low economic standard, there is betting. Macedonia is not a rich country, and ironically it has a huge betting culture. In the center of Ohrid's Carsija, every morning young football-obsessed people have a cheap coffee in the sports gambling bars, watch football and write gambling tickets for that day, consulting with the people around them if they've made the right choice by choosing which team will win at what time.

People can bet on every sport and every event, like new political party elections, Oscars, dog racing and every sport in the world. While it can be fun, this betting culture is a known problem that natives discuss among them.

Ohrid has become a home to a few well-known casinos, also, so if you are interested in coming to Ohrid and having a little bit of Monaco-like fun on a budget, then hit our Casinos – the drinks are free, and they characteristically are open 24/7.

20. As Safe As Houses

The Balkan is considered among the World's population as not being as safe as it should be, but the truth is that Ohrid is one of the safest cities in the World.

Stories about people forgetting their bags and finding them the day after at the same place are very common. You can wander the streets in Ohrid at 4 am and nobody will care, except some nervous old lady who will without hesitation drop a bucket of water on your head if you make a lot of noise.

Ohrid is an amazingly safe city with a very small criminal rate, so it is perfect for a family-friendly vacation.

21. Still Not Safe For The LGBTQ

The thing that we're not proud of as Macedonians, is that the gay population doesn't have any rights here. It is still a taboo topic here and many people still hide and don't express themselves and their sexual orientation fully and truly.

That is why I am obliged to warn you that even though I congratulate you on living as your most authentic self, maybe it is a good idea not to be as loud here as you would be in the streets of London, for example.

Macedonian people are slowly starting to get used to the queer people, but it is still very fresh and not completely accepted as the norm here.

22. Wear Whatever You Like

Ohrid is a mix of religions and cultures, but they are all accepting of the people's choice of clothes. If you don't plan on entering a religious building, then you can wear whatever you like. In the summer girls with bikinis and Birkenstocks and topless guys with shorts and flip flops are a common sight in the center, and despite being a small country, Macedonia is very fashion-forward and people try a lot to look put together and presentable.

23. Internet And Network

An interesting fact is that Macedonia is the first wireless country in the World. Having a lot of more advanced and rich countries in western Europe, the USAID still decided to give us the gift of a good Internet.

We have a great Internet connection and oftentimes every place has a very stable WiFi connection that is free to use for as long as you want. The only condition is, of course, to pay for some of the services they offer, like buying a coffee or eating a meal.

A VERY IMPORTANT TIP is: turn OFF your roaming! Macedonia is one of the most expensive countries to make and take phone calls from, so if you don't want to pay the amount of money that would take

>TOURIST

you to a vacation to the Maldives, then turn off the roaming of your phone.

24. Social Websites To Follow For Local News

Macedonians like Twitter a lot, so you can search what's trending with hashtag #Macedonia or #Ohrid on twitter. The most visited Web portal for Ohrid latest news, weather and events is called Ohrid News, and some of the news are translated into English too. If you can't figure it out, just copy the text and translate it onto Google translate. The Macedonian English translation on Google is not perfect but is good enough for everyone to know what exactly is written in Macedonian.

25. Radio Culture

Radio is still a very popular medium, especially for people who work in the offices and joggers. The most popular and award-winning radio station is called Super Radio 97.0 MHz FM. It plays contemporary music and also takes time each day to dedicate a few hours to some well known and loved world classics.

If you want to learn about traditional Folk music then turn on Lav Radio on 91.5 MHz, and you'll suddenly feel like a middle-aged drunk villager with marriage problems.

26. Music – What's Popular?

In Ohrid, people are drawn to different kinds of music, but the most popular local bars will play contemporary pop music, mixed with house elements. You will be surprised that the most iconic and visited two places are both called Jazz – only one is "Jazz Inn" and the other one is "Jazz and Blues". The first one is an amazing jazz bar in the old part of the town called Varosh, and the other one is a cabaret with live music almost every day that works until the sun comes up.

In the more traditional restaurants in the offseason, you will find a live band that will play traditional Macedonian songs that are called "old town". Oftentimes in these places, natives get emotional during some song and they would call the band to sing it close to their year, leaving them tips in their instruments sometimes as big as their months' salary.

In the summertime, you will find every single genre of music there is at the beach parties and numerous bars located all around Ohrid.

27. Art – What's Popular?

Wood-carving is the most popular and interesting art form in Ohrid. People have their workshops that you can visit and sometimes even order something you would like to be carved – the usual themes are religious figures like the Ohrid theologians Cyril and Methodius, or Saints Clement and Naum, their disciples.

There are a few amazing galleries that you can visit and see all kinds of Macedonian art. Watercolors and aquarelles are the most common styles, and romantic Ohrid scenery is the number one motif presented there. The art is quite expensive there, but the quality is second to none. The most popular gallery is Bukefal located on the main shopping street – Carsija.

If you want to buy something cute, but still artful, then head over to the old part of the town where you will find little shops where the owners handmake Ohrid themed and also modern themed items such as cups, magnets, shirts, bags, pictures, badges and other easy to carry objects. An interesting Atelier to visit is Aini, located in the center.

28. Jewelry – What's Popular?

The most popular to buy in Ohrid is the pearl – a unique, beautiful and historic, but I will tell you about the pearl in a separate paragraph. People in Ohrid love to make their own jewelry and you can find anything from wool necklaces to silver filigree, to pearl earrings. Depending on your taste I guarantee you that Ohrid is the place to buy good quality and unique jewelry. The Carsija is filled with pearl and stone jewelry, usually owned by the Turkish merchants who will offer you a good price for the item you would like to buy. Still, don't overdo it, remember the jewelry is of very good quality, so don't expect to get a very low price.

The filigree is a style of jewelry and art-making that involves the curving of silver wire into amazing pieces of wearable art. It is so popular in Ohrid that there are classes in the community college that can teach you the art of making filigree so you can pass it by generations. It is considered to be high-level craftsmanship and you must respect the price and the profession.

>TOURIST

29. The Almighty Pearl

Probably the most famous Ohrid product is the Ohrid pearl, jewelry that has not been even resisted by the British Queen Elizabeth. The very way of making is known only to members of certain families, and the secret has been successfully kept since the 1920s. The pearls are made from the scallop fish shells inherent in Lake Ohrid, and, interestingly, the 'recipe' for making is passed on only to male heirs. In fact, only two families make genuine, original Ohrid pearls. These are the Talev and Filev families. Talevi started the business in 1924 when they purchased a formula for the production of pearls in Russia. They procured the material in Bethlehem and started making it. To this day, they have retained manual production and work only with natural materials. You can find many pearl shops in town, but most of them are cheap copies or they are not made with the same ingredients as the Filev and Talev family pearls. If you are willing to spend a little more on a unique souvenir, necklace, earrings or the like, visit their Talev family and Filev family stores.

30. Shopping Culture

Ohrid is not a major shopping city, so if you are thinking of it as a low-budget Milano, think again. Although the Carsija is filled with clothing stores, you will not likely find original brands, except in the sports shops. This is due to Macedonia not being part of the European Union or any Union in particular, so the cost of getting brand clothes here for selling would be an absolute fortune for the merchants.

The biggest clothing retail shop in 2020 is Waikiki, where you can find interesting everyday pieces of clothing at a low cost. Interesting and unique clothes are available in the private clothing stores in the center, but remember, if you see a Versace blouse for a weird in-between price, don't buy it-it's a knock-off.

SUMMER:

31. Take A Swim

Oh, summer. The summers in Ohrid are what paradise must look like, except with a little bit of loud music and the occasional drunk teenager.

You will be making a sin if you don't visit any of the beaches available in Ohrid and the neighborhood.

>TOURIST

If you don't want to bother with public transport like a van or a bus and go a little bit further, there are a few beaches that are located right in the heart of the town that are just as great. The first and closest beach is called Saraishte, it is located at the beginning of the old part of town, very close to the iconic jazz bar called Jazz Inn. It is a small, stone beach that is filled with commoners and has lovely mini willow trees around it. If you continue to walk straight ahead and pass a small bridge left of the pretty church of st. Sofia, then you will get access to the three of the most beautiful beaches in Ohrid – Potpes, Kaneo (below the church of Kaneo) and Labino. The last one looks like a private beach, and has just recently gotten its popularity because the Ohrid local community has built a hiking trail that leads to it. People from Ohrid were quite disappointed because this hidden gem has been discovered by the tourists, but know the secret's out in the open, be sure you don't miss this beautiful beach.

If you decide to take some sort of vehicle to travel a longer distance, then you can hit the road that leads to the Albanian border. The beaches that you'll find sequentially on the road are Cuba Libre beach, Gorica 1,2, and 3, The Lagadin beaches, Peshtani village beach, the Gradiste beaches known for parties, Trpejca village beach, Ljubanista, and Saint Naum. All of these have a stone coast, except Ljubanista (Lew-bah-neesh-tah), which has sand among the stones. A beautiful mountain scenery will guide you on your way to the further beaches, so I guarantee you that you won't be bored.

32. TAXI AND OTHER TRANSPORT

Ohrid natives have a pretty complicated relationship with their taxi drivers. Be aware that the taxi prices go up in the summer and oftentimes taxi drivers refuse to take natives who will ask for a smaller distance than a tourist who'll like to go to Saint Naum, for example. My advice is to always ask for the taximeter to be on, and Google "Taxi Services in Ohrid", then dial those numbers. If you don't have a phone and you cannot call a taxi, then choose the taxis that have some sort of a name of a company on their plate. And ALWAYS ask for the driver to turn on the taximeter and tell you the approximate price before you start your journey. Taxi drivers are virtually the best local guides, so if you get blessed with a talkative and nice driver, then you will find out things about Ohrid that no guide book will tell you.

>TOURIST

    Another popular transportation in summer is the local bus that can also sometimes be a van. They have the last destination written on a nameplate on the windshield, and they make a stop at every bus stop in town. If you are not sure if the beach you want to go to is before or after the last destination written, and you don't have a way to Google it, then just ask anybody or the driver, and they will be happy to tell you which bus you need to take. The price is usually around 1 euro for the longest road for the van, and it should be around 3 and a half euros for 3 miles for the taxi fare.

33. Public Holidays

If you think about visiting Ohrid in the summertime, then my recommendation is to skip the public holiday Ilinden, which is celebrated on the 2nd of August. Republic Day or the Day of the Republic of Ilinden is a major national holiday in Macedonia. It is also a major religious holiday – Ilinden (St. Elijah day). This is considered to be the most crowded day in the whole year, as it is in the heat of the season. The Ohrid season is considered to reach its peak from the 20th of July until the 20th of August, and all the major events are packed in this month. If you are not interested in big concerts or electronic music parties, then it's better not to visit Ohrid on the 1st or 2nd of August – finding an available accommodation will be a nightmare and the beaches are stacked with tourists.

34. Parties

A city with an amazing cultural and educational history, Ohrid can still be a party city if you decide to visit it in July and August. The weather is so warm and pleasant, that there are a lot of open-air parties that usually last until sunrise. Gradiste 1,2 and 3 beaches, also called Orevche and Bane are one of the most popular ones for trance and hip hop parties. Orevce also hosts the annual cinema festival which is free to enter and you can watch European movies by the lake on comfortable pillows, drinking cold Macedonian beer.

The biggest concerts and music festivals are saved for the week around 2nd of August – The 4 day long Ohrid Calling filled with world-famous DJs, the Ohrid summer festival for classical music and theater, and individual concerts are all happening that week. It is crazy and exciting at the same time.

35. Experience The Lake – Rent a Kayak

If you take a stroll around the Ohrid Riviera then you'll notice people kayaking. You can do this also if you want to have a more private experience discovering the beauty of the lake. You can rent a kayak or a paddle board also called a SUP on the Potpes beach, and you will be amazed by how intimate and nature-bonding this experience can be. The Ohrid lake is sometimes behaving like a sea due to its maximum depth of 288 m (940 ft), making it one of the deepest lakes in the world, so if you see some waves, then maybe skip this one. If you know how to swim there is absolutely no risk in kayaking near the bay because it is a very shallow area, but you will most definitely soak completely in water if you choose to kayak or to board when the lake is wavy.

36. What To Take With You – Clothes

The average temperatures in Ohrid in summer are around 85 Fahrenheit, and the evenings are around 60 F. So If you come here in the summertime – Take your summer dresses and bikini for the day, linen clothes are a must as Ohrid and Macedonia are sunny places. There is a pleasant gust of wind almost every day because of the fresh lake, something that you won't find in the crowdy Skopje, for example. The heat is always manageable and if things get out of control, you have an amazing lake you can freshen up in. For the evenings you can just take a jean jacket or some cardigan, and jeans are welcomed, but maybe not in August, when it's usually the hottest. Sandals, flip flops, and light closed-toe shoes are a nice option. Just, please don't wear flip flops when you go out eating or clubbing, the natives will give you a disgusted look as they like to look put together and classy.

>TOURIST

37. What To Take With You – Items

Traveling on your own with a car often means that you can take food and groceries from your home country to maybe save some money. The thing is that in Ohrid there is so much cheap food in the restaurant and in the markets that you don't have to do this. Other items I don't think you should take are swimming mattresses or inflatable balls, as you can find them here in all stores for a very cheap price of 3-10 euros. Take your chargers which should have a European adapter, and maybe take some water-resistant camera like a go pro, so you get a chance to take amazing underwater pictures and videos.

38. What To Photograph

The moment you arrive in Ohrid it will be clear to you that this is one of the cutest and photogenic places you'll ever visit. The most popular photos are taken at the Church of Saint John of Kaneo, a church located on the coast of the hill of the old part of the town. It overlooks the whole lake and the mountains surrounding it, and it's conveniently close to the center, only 15 minutes walking and you're there. The other popular place to have a photo is up to the Samuel's Fortress, a massive ruin of magnificent walls that crown the city hill, which is located 5 minutes up the hill from the Kaneo church. Climbing up the Fortress you will notice that the whole town looks like it is in your hands.

Another good idea if you want to take good photos is to wait for the sunset on any beach in Ohrid. The sunsets on the Albanian side so you'll always see a breathtaking reflection of the Sun in the Lake when it sets.

If you are interested in hiking then go up the village called Velestovo. It is on the way to the mountain Galicica and from there you can see Ohrid from a different angle. Instead of climbing up the Samuel Fortress and seeing Ohrid from the old-town hill, from Velestovo you can see Ohrid, the Lake, and the Hill together with the scenic Fortress.

39. Festivals

Along with the great parties available in the summertime, Ohrid offers three festivals that are created for the more serious, grown-up people who are not particularly interested in loud music and partying.

>TOURIST

The "Balkan Festival of folk songs and dances" is an international folklore event established in 1962. It is a host of dozens of dance assemblies from all over Europe, who showcase their traditional dance and clothes. It is located in a small park in the heart of Ohrid, next to the Carsija.

The Ohrid Summer Festival (Ohridsko Leto) is a festival founded on 4 August 1961, always taking place between 12 July and 20 August. Many world-renowned musicians like Leonid Kogan, Svyatoslav Richter, Grigory Sokolov, Andre Navarra, Martina Arroyo, Henryk Szeryng, Ivo Pogorelić, Mstislav Rostropovich, Aldo Ciccolini, Gidon Kremer, Ruggiero Ricci, Viktor Tretiakov, Salvatore Accardo, Elena Obraztsova, Katia Ricciarelli, Victoria de Los Ángeles, Maxim Vengerov, Vadim Repin, Julian Rachlin, Michel Camilo, Paul Meyer, Dmitri Hvorostovsky, Leo Nucci, Barbara Frittoli, Jessye Norman, Nigel Kennedy, Zubin Mehta, Ennio Morricone, Mikhail Pletnev and many other have performed at Ohridsko Leto. This festival also hosts popular theater and opera plays, so if you're not a fan of music but like a bit of drama, you can find it at Ohridsko Leto.

Ohridski Trubaduri - Ohrid Fest is a music festival that takes place every summer at the beginning of the month of July. It began in 1994 as a showcase for

Macedonian summer folklore. In 1997, a pop evening was introduced to motivate Macedonian lyricists and composers, as well as artists. It lasts three days – The first day is for folk music, the second for Macedonian pop and the last is international and it commonly features a popular Balkan star as a guest star.

40. Sports

Ribari (Fishermen) is the official Ohrid club for sports supporters, who are very dedicated and passionate about the teams that originate from Ohrid. Handball is arguably the most popular and successful sport.

Basket (basketball with only one hoop) is the most popular neighborhood sport played by young and old people, as a sort of a socializing game and it is very common to have a basketball court in a lot of the city's neighborhoods.

Although we have this amazing lake, weirdly enough, there is a shortage of training pools in the city, so swimming is not a sport that we excel in, but we do host an amazing sports event. The Ohrid Swimming Marathon is an international Open water swimming competition. It`s held once a year in the waters of Ohrid

Lake, usually taking place on the 19th of August. The swimming path "Klime Savin" is 30 km (18.4 miles) long starting from the Monastery of St. Naum and going north toward the city port of Ohrid.

Another sport event you can be a part of which is a "little bit" easier, is a fairly new but popular traditional running marathon (5k and 10k) called Ohrid Trchat (Ohrid Runs, said in Ohrid dialect), which takes place on the streets in the Ohrid center. It is of a humanitarian nature and a lot of people from Ohrid train for it running by the Ohrid coast.

WINTER (OFF-SEASON)

41. Experience The Mountains – Hike

Hike through the mountains to visit an ancient cave church or a traditional village like Velestovo or Elshani where time seems to doesn't exist. Hike to the peak of Galicica for a breathtaking view, or go to Konjsko village and have a hearty traditional meal at the tavern there. If you are not as fit as a horse, then simply walking up the hill in the old part of the town is a little bit of an exercise as well. If you want to reach the most popular church of Kaneo, then don't take the bridge, go up the hill and climb down again. The roads are very safe as the old town is populated and the evenings are romantically lit by traditional street light with yellow undertones.

42. IF YOU GET UP EARLY

Ohrid likes to sleep. As Macedonia is a slow-paced country, and people's jobs are usually on a walking distance from their own home, the locals like to sleep until they must get up. So, if you are used to getting up very early, be aware that there is a possibility that nothing will be open. As the stores usually open at 9 am, you will see only yellow uniforms of the local cleaning company, in the empty parks, who clean the city tirelessly in the waking hours of 5-7 am. But that means that you have the whole city by yourself! If you are an early bird, then hang out with the real early birds. Go by the lake, and prepare a snack from the night before, like a sandwich or chips. Prepare to share it with the always hungry seagulls and swans, and think of yourself as being the lead actor in a romantic scene.

>TOURIST

43. An Idea If You Want To Take A Swim

In the off-season months, if you are Russian or Scandinavian you can enjoy a swim and have a blast. But if you come from a warmer country, swimming in the lake is an absolute no-no. There is a way you can merge hiking and swimming in colder weather, too. I recommend you to take your backpack with your swimwear, put on some music or a podcast to listen to, and start walking by the Ohrid Riviera until you get to Gorica 2 beach. There is a hotel called Inex Olgica where you can pay for a 24-hour card, which includes a pool with a lake view, sauna, gym, and massage. You can also have a drink there and after a few hours when you are completely dry and relax you can get back to your place on the same route.

44. Where Is The Most Breathtaking View

Views, views, views. If you search for Ohrid online, you will see the word "view" everywhere, because it really is full of wonderful scenery.

For me, for example, if the view contains only the lake, I can get quite depressed, because it looks a little bit melancholic. On the other side, if I only see the town, yes, it is a lovely town, but it is not that unique. The best view is if I can have a little bit of everything.

In Ohrid, it is considered that the best view of the town is on the balcony of a villa in the center called Tabana. It is an open balcony where a lot of people book rooms with a view to enjoy the mixed picture of the lake, port and the city center. On top of the villa, there is a big terrace where locals usually go to watch the biggest holiday in the winter – Vodici (Epiphany). The owners will serve you hot rakia for free, as per tradition.

45. Vodici – the most important day for locals

Vodici, or Epiphany - the day on which according to Christian tradition St. John the Baptist baptized Jesus Christ into the Jordan River. It is celebrated on January 19th at churches using the Julian calendar (including the Macedonian one) and on January 7th at churches using the Gregorian calendar). This gives importance to baptism as one of the most sacred secrets of Christianity. People from all over the world gather to see which person from the locals will catch the sacred cross thrown in the lake by a holy person. The person who will catch the cross guides it in his home until the next year, and together with his friends sings the traditional song "Vo Yordanie", while waiting for the locals to give him money, a simple gesture of congratulations. The people who were born in Ohrid are all amazing divers and swimmers, and they resemble dolphins when swimming in the lake in such low temperatures. Free hot rakia (fruit brandy) is served everywhere, and people celebrate this day with music, dancing and of course, drinking.

46. Explore The Neighbourhood

Ohrid in winter can be quite dull, as the day is short, and the sunsets at around 4.30 pm. This is a great opportunity to take a bus, taxi, or your car and head to Bitola, an iconic Macedonian city known for its century-long importance in the realm of diplomacy, and also its unprecedented top café-culture. It is a city with a long street filled with cafes, called Sirok Sokak (Wide Street), where you can find a punker having a coffee with an elderly man, and fashion-forward girls having a chuckle over big macchiatos.

Ohrid currently doesn't have a cinema that shows movie projections, and its cultural center called Gligor Prlicev is mainly used for theater plays and the very popular comedy improv show called Improvokacija, which resembles the popular show Whose Line Is It Anyway.

You can use the trip to Bitola to watch the latest blockbusters in the Culture Center 3D Cinema, which is located directly on the Sirok Sokak in the heart of town.

47. The Village With Its Own

>TOURIST

Passport

A visit to the village called Vevchani is an amazing idea throughout the whole year. It is located around the closest town in Ohrid called Struga, sitting on a hill and home of lovely springs, a church, and a multitude of amazing traditional restaurants that serve traditional food along with oldtown music.

In the warmer off-season months, you can arrange for horse-riding in the lovely woods of Vevcani, and the winter is saved for the Vevcani Carnival. Held traditionally from 12-14 of January, it celebrates the arrival of the New Year according to the old calendar. It is a masquerade at which the locals dress up in hand-made costumes to satirically depict the current political events in the country and the world. It is, of course, filled with music and alcohol, the main drinks being a rakia and vino (wine). In 1993 the Carnival and the village of Vevcani officially became part of the World Federation of Carnival Cities. In recent years a special "Carnival Passport" has been issued at the Carnival.

48. Museums

You can learn a lot about a city if you visit its museums in the old part of the town of Varos. Going to the National Workshop For Handmade Paper is a must - one of the seventh in the World in which the paper is made in the original Chinese way from Second Century BC. The method is unique and it revives the old tradition in Ohrid.

Next to it is the very famous museum in the House of Robevci, one of the richest and most influential families in Ohrid. Furnished with paintings, maps, clothes, and costumes, it is an interesting overview of how middle-class families used to live.

A few minutes away is the Icon Gallery next to the Church of Mother of Perivlepta. Containing mainly beautifully painted icons with gold details from the 14 century, this little icon gallery should not be missed if you love art. As it is located in the upper part of the old city, after your visit you can walk down to the lake and have a coffee in some of the bars on the coast.

>TOURIST

49. Visit The Fishermen

After you have your coffee, you can walk by the riviera and visit the fishermen. It is an amazing view to picture as they are usually old friends with the same passion who calmly wait for the fish to catch bait. This sport is usually accompanied by their pet dogs, radio and drinks, and it can last until the morning. Fishing is legal only a few months of the year and if you get here in the spring, you can buy a fishing ticket and join them. You will learn so much about the flora and fauna in the lake, directly from the experts.

50. Never Get Sick Again – The Happy Meal For Grown-ups

I intentionally left this tip to be the last, as it is the most important one of the bunch. If you are here for one day, one week, one month, doesn't matter. What matters is to always find time for the Adult Happy meal – Corba (the middle road between a soup and stew), Rakia and Garlic spread. This traditional breakfast is the recipe for health and the reason why you can smell the garlic among the locals in the morning hours.

The traditional restaurants and lounge bars will serve you a chorba of your own choice – the most common are calf, fish, and vegetables. The most hard-core choice is the Chkembe, but it's not for everybody, as it is made from the inside edible lining of various animals, also known as tripe. It is considered to be a great hangover remedy, which is ironic as it is oftentimes served with a glass of rakia. The garlic spread is traditionally made only with garlic and vinegar and it has a liquid form that you pour into the soup, but nowadays most of the restaurants opt for a garlic spread that has looks like a paste and you can put it on a piece of homemade bread.

Be careful as this is considered to be a breakfast meal, you can meet a shortage of chorba if you ask for it in the afternoon. When you have this hearty meal you will be glad to compensate a few hours of your sleep for the delicious, warm stew in your belly.

>TOURIST

TOP REASONS TO BOOK THIS TRIP

Lake and Beaches: I dare you to find better beaches in Macedonia. Amazing in the summer for parties and swimming, breathtaking for camping and waiting for the sunset in the offseason.

Although we are not a country that has a sea or an ocean, our lake is one of the oldest and deepest lakes in the world, and it behaves and looks just like a sea. When the wind breaks loose you can see waves as tall as a building, and its deep green color gives a mistic feel that will make you think it is full of ancient secrets.

Food: Macedonian food is amazing. Heavily influenced by Turkish cuisine, the Macedonian and Balkan foods are meat and vegetable-heavy, offering you meals that will warm your heart and belly, but don't leave you so full that you will feel like puking. Always made with love and home-grown vegetables, fruits and spices, you won't find any cuisine like ours anywhere in the world.

The calm: When tourists come here and they experience the rich culture and amazing beaches, they say they love it. But, you can find amazing culture and lovely beaches everywhere in the world. Tourists say that they can imagine themselves living here for another reason besides these. The calmness Ohrid exudes is out of this world. It has a spirit of its own, and people choose it to spend the rest of their lives here because they all say that it is soul-enriching and nerve-saving. In this stress-inducing world that we live in right now, having a city like Ohrid in this small, sunny country called Macedonia is truly a priceless gift.

\>TOURIST

Did you Know?

The old part of the town called Varos has roads that are built with old stones. The Carsija was recently replaced with modern tiles, with the disapproval of the locals. The old stone road that is so charming is called Kaldrma.

Last practical piece of advice for car drivers:
Ohrid is a city that contains both new and old parts. The Old part called Varosh is a small hill filled with small narrow streets that are pretty hard to navigate if you are not an experienced driver. If you book accommodation in the heart of the city, the center or the old part, be prepared that even though they offer parking places, they cannot guarantee the availability. It is a common situation that a parking place is taken over by a local who left the car in the parking lot without asking the owner for permission.

If something like this happens to you, don't despair and park in the city parking lot. The day card is cheap and it is a convenient place to leave your car as it is close to everything.

OTHER RESOURCES:

The most popular web portal in Ohrid https://www.ohridnews.com -

Information for Hiking trails in Ohrid https://www.wikiloc.com/trails/hiking/macedonia/ohrid -

Information on legitimate taxis in Ohrid and their phone numbers https://zk.mk/taksi-kompanii/ohrid?lang=en -

Emergency phone numbers:

Firebrigade:+389193

Police: +389192

Ambulance: +389194

Eco-line: +38970236000

Electro distribution:+38989088888

AMSM- telephone for roadside assistance and towage: +389196

>TOURIST

Packing and Planning Tips

A Week before Leaving

- Arrange for someone to take care of pets and water plants.
- Email and Print important Documents.
- Get Visa and vaccines if needed.
- Check for travel warnings.
- Stop mail and newspaper.
- Notify Credit Card companies where you are going.
- Passports and photo identification is up to date.
- Pay bills.
- Copy important items and download travel Apps.
- Start collecting small bills for tips.
- Have post office hold mail while you are away.
- Check weather for the week.
- Car inspected, oil is changed, and tires have the correct pressure.
- Check airline luggage restrictions.
- Download Apps needed for your trip.

Right Before Leaving

- Contact bank and credit cards to tell them your location.
- Clean out refrigerator.
- Empty garbage cans.
- Lock windows.
- Make sure you have the proper identification with you.
- Bring cash for tips.
- Remember travel documents.
- Lock door behind you.
- Remember wallet.
- Unplug items in house and pack chargers.
- Change your thermostat settings.
- Charge electronics, and prepare camera memory cards.

\>TOURIST

READ OTHER GREATER THAN A TOURIST BOOKS

Greater Than a Tourist- Geneva Switzerland: 50 Travel Tips from a Local by Amalia Kartika

Greater Than a Tourist- St. Croix US Birgin Islands USA: 50 Travel Tips from a Local by Tracy Birdsall

Greater Than a Tourist- San Juan Puerto Rico: 50 Travel Tips from a Local by Melissa Tait

Greater Than a Tourist – Lake George Area New York USA: 50 Travel Tips from a Local by Janine Hirschklau

Greater Than a Tourist – Monterey California United States: 50 Travel Tips from a Local by Katie Begley

Greater Than a Tourist – Chanai Crete Greece: 50 Travel Tips from a Local by Dimitra Papagrigoraki

Greater Than a Tourist – The Garden Route Western Cape Province South Africa: 50 Travel Tips from a Local by Li-Anne McGregor van Aardt

Greater Than a Tourist – Sevilla Andalusia Spain: 50 Travel Tips from a Local by Gabi Gazon

Children's Book: *Charlie the Cavalier Travels the World* by Lisa Rusczyk Ed. D.

> TOURIST

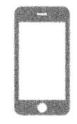

Follow us on Instagram for beautiful travel images:
http://Instagram.com/GreaterThanATourist

Follow *Greater Than a Tourist* on Amazon.
>Tourist Podcast
>T Website
>T Youtube
>T Facebook
>T Goodreads
>T Amazon
>T Mailing List
>T Pinterest
>T Instagram
>T Twitter
>T SoundCloud
>T LinkedIn
>T Map

> TOURIST

At *Greater Than a Tourist*, we love to share travel tips with you. How did we do? What guidance do you have for how we can give you better advice for your next trip? Please send your feedback to GreaterThanaTourist@gmail.com as we continue to improve the series. We appreciate your constructive feedback. Thank you.

>TOURIST

METRIC CONVERSIONS

TEMPERATURE

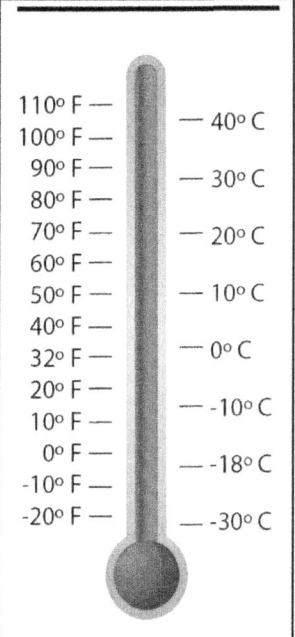

110° F — — 40° C
100° F —
90° F — — 30° C
80° F —
70° F — — 20° C
60° F —
50° F — — 10° C
40° F —
32° F — — 0° C
20° F —
10° F — — -10° C
0° F —
 — -18° C
-10° F —
-20° F — — -30° C

To convert F to C:

Subtract 32, and then multiply by 5/9 or .5555.

To Convert C to F:
Multiply by 1.8
and then add 32.

32F = 0C

LIQUID VOLUME

To Convert:................Multiply by
U.S. Gallons to Liters................. 3.8
U.S. Liters to Gallons 26
Imperial Gallons to U.S. Gallons 1.2
Imperial Gallons to Liters....... 4.55
Liters to Imperial Gallons 22
1 Liter = .26 U.S. Gallon
1 U.S. Gallon = 3.8 Liters

DISTANCE

To convert ....Multiply by
Inches to Centimeters 2.54
Centimeters to Inches 39
Feet to Meters....................... .3
Meters to Feet 3.28
Yards to Meters 91
Meters to Yards 1.09
Miles to Kilometers 1.61
Kilometers to Miles............ .62
1 Mile = 1.6 km
1 km = .62 Miles

WEIGHT

1 Ounce = .28 Grams
1 Pound = .4555 Kilograms
1 Gram = .04 Ounce
1 Kilogram = 2.2 Pounds

73

>TOURIST

Travel Questions

- Do you bring presents home to family or friends after a vacation?
- Do you get motion sick?
- Do you have a favorite billboard?
- Do you know what to do if there is a flat tire?
- Do you like a sun roof open?
- Do you like to eat in the car?
- Do you like to wear sun glasses in the car?
- Do you like toppings on your ice cream?
- Do you use public bathrooms?
- Did you bring a cell phone and does it have power?
- Do you have a form of identification with you?
- Have you ever been pulled over by a cop?
- Have you ever given money to a stranger on a road trip?
- Have you ever taken a road trip with animals?
- Have you ever gone on a vacation alone?
- Have you ever run out of gas?
- If you could move to any place in the world, where would it be?

- If you could travel anywhere in the world, where would you travel?
- If you could travel in any vehicle, which one would it be?
- If you had three things to wish for from a magic genie, what would they be?
- If you have a driver's license, how many times did it take you to pass the test?
- What are you the most afraid of on vacation?
- What do you want to get away from the most when you are on vacation?
- What foods smell bad to you?
- What item do you bring on ever trip with you away from home?
- What makes you sleepy?
- What song would you love to hear on the radio when you're cruising on the highway?
- What travel job would you want the least?
- What will you miss most while you are away from home?
- What is something you always wanted to try?
- What is the best road side attraction that you ever saw?
- What is the farthest distance you ever biked?

>TOURIST

- What is the farthest distance you ever walked?
- What is the weirdest thing you needed to buy while on vacation?
- What is your favorite candy?
- What is your favorite color car?
- What is your favorite family vacation?
- What is your favorite food?
- What is your favorite gas station drink or food?
- What is your favorite license plate design?
- What is your favorite restaurant?
- What is your favorite smell?
- What is your favorite song?
- What is your favorite sound that nature makes?
- What is your favorite thing to bring home from a vacation?
- What is your favorite vacation with friends?
- What is your favorite way to relax?
- Where is the farthest place you ever traveled in a car?
- Where is the farthest place you ever went North, South, East and West?
- Where is your favorite place in the world?

- Who is your favorite singer?
- Who taught you how to drive?
- Who will you miss the most while you are away?
- Who if the first person you will contact when you get to your destination?
- Who brought you on your first vacation?
- Who likes to travel the most in your life?
- Would you rather be hot or cold?
- Would you rather drive above, below, or at the speed limited?
- Would you rather drive on a highway or a back road?
- Would you rather go on a train or a boat?
- Would you rather go to the beach or the woods?

>TOURIST

Travel Bucket List

1.

2.

3.

4.

5.

6.

7.

8.

9.

10.

>TOURIST

NOTES

Printed in Great Britain
by Amazon